Sonnets about Serial Killers

Sonnets About Serial Killers
© 2013 by Somtow Sucharitkul
published by Diplodocus Press
Los Angeles • Bangkok
All Rights Reserved

First Edition

10 9 8 7 6 5 4 3 2 1

The poems "Jeffrey Dahmer" and "In Praise of Entropy" originally appeared in the anthology *Once Upon a Midnight*, published by Unnameable Press, 1995

ISBN
Hardcover 978-0-9800149-3-8
Trade Paperback 978-0-9860533-5-1

Sonnets about Serial killers

by

S.P. Somtow

DIPLODOCUS PRESS
BANGKOK • LOS ANGELES

Disclaimer

Poetry, they say is truth. Certainly, poets believe this.

However, the legal definition of truth makes no provision for poetic license, and in any case, mine will probably be revoked as soon as this book is published.

It is therefore necessary to preface this book with the usual fiction disclaimer:

This is a work of fiction. Well, of course it is. Real people don't go around speaking in iambic pentameter. So, obviously, the things in this book didn't happen. Well, similar things may have happened to people with identical names, but these names, and these events, are used fictitiously. Any resemblance to persons living, dead, undead, or not yet born, or events that might have happened to such persons, is decidedly coincidental.

I wasn't there, I didn't see anything. I lied. Let's leave it at that.

Deification

*To Michael Meredith,
who taught me everything about
what poetry is —
and what it isn't*

Contents

The Argument
Introductory Words

I: Serial Killers
    Ed Gein
    Ed Gein Critiques his Biopics
    Jeffrey Dahmer
    John Wayne Gacy
    On a List of People at One Time Thought to be
        Jack the Ripper
    Armin Meiwes: The Cannibal
    Albert Fish

II: Gay Bible Stories
    Tinky Winky at the Televangelist's Tomb
    Matthew Shepard

III: Women Who Kill Their Own Children
    Andrea Yates: On Drowning my Babies
    Susan Smith: On Driving my Babies to the Lake
    Dena Schlosser: On Slicing Off my Baby's Arms

IV: Mass Murderers
    Blacksburg
    Columbine

V: Children Who Kill Their Parents
    Alex King
    The Menendez Brothers

VI: Washington, DC
    The Lewinsky Quartet:
        Monica Lewinsky
        To a Cigar
        On a Copy of Leaves of Grass
            Presented by the President
            to Miss Lewinsky
    The Sky at Night
    A Congressional Page Contemplates
        Mr. Foley's Proposition
    Mr. Foley Contemplates the Internet

VII: Science Fiction
    In Praise of Entropy

VIII: Silly Sonnets on Serious Subjects
    Moral Ambiguity in Thailand and Sudan
    On Looking into a Copy of Chapman's Homer
        that Might Have Belonged to Keats
    George Junius Stinney
    A Prime Example of Why the Sonnet is not the Ideal
        Medium for the lyrics of Popular Music

Appendix
    The Italians

End Notes
    The Historical Context

Sonnets about Serial Killers

The Argument

Be scared, my friends. Be very,
    very scared.
This book will take you from the
    paths you've known,

To sights unseen, dark corners
    never bared,
To deeds undared, halls never
braved alone.
Forget the world of Spenser's airy Faerie
Shakespeare's bisexual angst, or Petrarch's passion;
This poet's cream's decidedly non-dairy,
His skewed perspective somewhat *not* the fashion.

To this poetic banquet do I bring
Inquiring minds that have inquired too much:
Of Court TV and Tabloids do I sing,
Of killers, perverts, hypocrites, and such,
For in life's drama, they too play their part.
Inhuman horror hides a human heart.

Introductory Words

Many far greater poets than I have scaled all the possible heights that the sonnet could possibly scale. In this little book, it is my intention to plumb the depths.

It is not as shocking a stratagem as you might imagine. I have always believed that a proper understanding of the sublime is always based on a firm grounding in the sublunary. Before Jesus ascended into Heaven, according to the Apostle's Creed, "he descended into Hell." The Harrowing of Hell, an event much depicted in Mediaeval literature, seems to have disappeared from the radar of contemporary faith, but from a mythic point of view it is an absolutely essential stop in the hero's journey (and the heroine's, for that matter). Whether you are Hercules, Orpheus, Luke Skywalker, or Savitri, you must, at some point in your quest for redemption, face that which is most dark about yourself.

There are several reasons why people today do not sit around tossing off sonnets at the dinner table. In this short essay I'm going to explain some of these reasons, and I'm also going to talk about why a writer of "cult fiction" and composer of operas has had a lifelong obsession with revivifying this art form.

It does seem ridiculous, doesn't it?

And yet I wonder whether I might not be able to do for the sonnet what my late colleague and mentor, Isaac Asimov, did for the limerick along with his co-conspirator, the brilliant John Ciardi.

It has come as a bit of a shock to me that many of my young friends don't exactly know what a sonnet is. Some have never read one. So, just the little essential potted factoids....

Sonnets have fourteen lines, and they are in iambic pentameter.

You've lost me already? Iambic pentameter is a line of poetry consisting of five *feet*. A foot is a unit of verse. The kind of feet used in iambic pentameter is the *iamb*, which is basically one unstressed syllable followed by a stressed one:

da DA da DA da DA da DA da DA.

Okay, but that's only the beginning, because the above is not intended as a rigid mandate. Poets are supposed to vary the rhythm from time to time with other kinds of feet. The most common other kinds used in the sonnet are the *trochee*, where the stress and unstress are reversed, the *anapest*, which has two unstressed syllables followed by a stressed one, and the *spondee,* which has both syllables being stressed.

You must combine this with the fact that the English language doesn't only have stressed and unstressed syllables. There are also medium stressed syllables, extremely stressed syllables, and long and short syllables. There is also the so-called *feminine ending,* where an extra unstressed syllable is added to the last foot. ("To be or not to be, that is the question.") To write decent iambic pentameter you must learn to play with all these variations, or the poem will be as bland and featureless as a disco remix.

Then, too, one must get rid of the idea that a line of verse must equal a line of content. Early examples of iambic pentameter did indeed follow this pattern, with a clear semantic break at the end of each line (the lines were known as "end-stopp'd") but it soon became more fun to run sentences across line endings ("enjambement") or put dramatic pauses in the middle.

With all these varieties, then, what is the bottom line? The bottom line is *five feet per line.* Everything else is negotiable. (French sonnets tend to be in six-foot lines or alexandrines; the pattern seems to fit the French language more naturally.) To see how far away you can get from da-DA da-DA and still be a sonnet, see Gerard Manley Hopkins's sonnet *The Windhover,* which uses a completely revolutionary stress system called *sprung rhythm,* yet still has five feet in each line.

In addition to the five-stress requirement, sonnets also have a rhyme scheme.

Now, the sonnet first became big in Italy, and in Italian *everything* rhymes. So, the sonnets of Petrarch, the first really famous practitioner of the form, used only a few rhymes throughout the poem. The first eight lines usually had the pattern *abbaabba,* and the last six *cdecde*. The Italian sonnet fell naturally into two complementary sections, the *octave* and the *sestet*. Often, the second section was a commentary on the first, a response to it, or otherwise formed a natural, asymmetrical coupling with the first.

When the art form reached England, it developed into a native English form which people call the Shakespearean sonnet (though he didn't invent it) because his sonnets are so well known. The rhyme scheme is *abab cdcd efef gg*. This made the sonnet almost like a mini-essay, in which three points are made and rounded off with a snappy conclusion.

But the rhyme scheme, like the da-Da da-DA pattern, isn't set in stone either. You can actually have any rhyme scheme you want, and W.H. Auden even wrote sonnets that didn't rhyme, though maybe that's going a bit too far.

In the final analysis, it's a sonnet if it's a sonnet.

The most important thing in all this is that the sonnet presents a very interesting balance between formal discipline and creative freedom. You only have fourteen lines in which to present your argument. Every stroke must count. Every rhythmic variation must have a purpose. And a sonnet must have something to say, because when you choose to use this form, you are strongly implying that what you have to say is important enough to be said in this form.

My own fixation with this art form comes from childhood. I became aware of the sonnet, I believe, when I was about 11, when I happened to read Oscar Wilde's story *A Portrait of Mr. W.H.*, in which the theory is propounded that

Shakespeare's sonnets were really written about a young boy actor named Willie Hughes. I must have been at least that young because at the age of twelve I read about the facts of life in a biology textbook, whereas I know that the various metrosexual complexities of Shakespeare's love life, blatantly implied in the short story, were all completely lost on me. All I know is that I fell in love with the form, the fourteen-line constraint of it, the fourteen-bar prison which must contain a universe of contemplation.

I immediately set about writing my own set, but I had not yet really grasped the notion that one sonnet must be a world unto itself. Not being mature enough to squeeze it into one, I made, instead, a determined effort to tell the mythical story of the Curse of the House of Atreus in an endless sequence of sonnets. I wrote over a hundred in a week or so. In fact, I was sure that I could have a sonnet sequence longer than Shakespeare's, so quantity, not quality was the object of the exercise.

Years later, having already established myself as a science fiction and fantasy writer of some notoriety, I was having an argument with a friend who told me unequivocally that the sonnet was dead.

That got my gander up because I love sonnets. But he did have a point.

In the heyday of the sonnet, there were many more possible grammatical permutations. For instance, you could say, *he talketh, he talks, he does talk, he doth talk,* all as reasonable variants, allowing much more freedom in arranging your words to fit the five-stress line. Words like *nation* could be pronounced as two syllables or three, again giving far more freedom in prosody.

Furthermore, the cornucopia of classical reference, the casual use of litotes, syncope, and conceited imagery, and the fashion for extravagantly inventive turns of phrase seemed to have all dissipated. Most hideously of all, the practice of penning an original poem to send to your girlfriend, patron, or mother had been hijacked by the people at Hallmark.

There had to be a way to fix that flatline.

The first job, then was to repair the notion that iambic pentameter was dead. In fact, from the prose of Theodore Sturgeon to the obscene blandishments of rap artists, the five-stress line is still very much the natural rhythm of the English language.

Consider the following vernacular utterances, which can be heard on any street in L.A. today:

"Oh, you just saying dat because we black."
"You think I give a shit about your problems?"
"Fuck you and you and you and you and you."
"A cheeseburger, small French fries, and a Coke."

Do you hear it? If Shakespeare were alive today....

Every single day of our lives, we hear lines of iambic pentameter and, whenever we speak English, we produce them.

The first step in reinventing the sonnet, then, is to reclaim the richness of our linguistic heritage.

What heritage? I hear the protests. Surely the vulgar sentences quoted above have nothing to do with Shakespeare and Milton!

But of course, they do. There are trillions and trillions of possible ways that words can connect, and each connection forms part of the great cosmic wheel of language. Poetry is not about the words themselves; it is about what you make them do. A poet must never forget that language is not his master. The language works for you, and never the reverse. If the language has not the means to say that which you are impelled to say, then it is up to you to bend the language to your will, to teach it tricks, force it to do your bidding.

The second step was to find something to say. Certainly the sexual cavortings of Zeus have less to say to today's audiences than they used to. Also, there's a lot less angst associated with, say, adulterous passions than there used to be, since people are a lot less concerned than they used to be about imminent damnation.

If there's no more mythology, and love has been preempted by MTV, what is there to write about?

This is where the tabloids come in.

There *is* a mythology today. We *do* have a shared matrix of stories that define the human condition. However, they are not to be found in Homer anymore. It is not Zeus but rather Elvis who has been spotted in a crowd. It is not Oedipus but rather President Clinton or Congressman Foley who have experienced a tragic flaw and fallen from grace. It is not Achilles who kills with passion and heroism, but Jeffrey Dahmer, with lust and secrecy.

It is my belief that it is only by digging in the sewer that we may ultimately locate the pearl of great price. And so this book of sonnets is a journey through some of humanity's less exalted moments. After all, though we may not want to admit it, serial killers share almost 100% of our DNA. We are cousins to gay-bashing bigots, schoolyard shootists, and philandering politicians. Certainly there is much dark humor in what you are about to read, but if can't laugh about some things, we might as well kill ourselves. Jerry Springer is our Virgil, guiding us through an inferno we have created ourselves, since we no longer believe in God.

So finally comes the third step. After finding a language of discourse, after finding a subject worthy of such a discourse, comes the discourse itself.

I shall prevaricate no longer.

Gentle reader ...

I

Serial Killers

Jeffrey Dahmer

Death is a little pinprick. Just a jab.
Nothing to fear. No suffering. No pain
Compared to the stern, stupefying stab
Of loneliness. Some acid to the brain
Will melt away that lingering abhorrence;
Then, all at once, by fiat from above,
Transcendence; for we'll taste tempestuous
               torrents
Of desire. For you, eternal love;
For me, mere transience; for I consume
And what was beautiful becomes old bones
And flesh, and rots in a suburban room,
While your response to my perfervid moans
Is not to speak at all. Oh stay, oh stay --
Not like the rest -- True love does not decay!

Ed Gein

A woman's privates stretched over his
                    own,
Her flayed paps strapped onto his manly chest,
He danced. With ornaments of womanbone
Clattering, tinkling; and with robes of dressed
And burnished womanskin, he danced. Alone
Under a dead Wisconsin moon, he danced,
Morphing himself through maiden, mother,
                    crone,
His drab droll being lightning-like enhanced
With a profound old magic, that outshone
Logic. But in this dancing, what can *we* perceive?
Could we too dance, though we be turned to
                    stone
By all that forces us to love, laugh, grieve,
Weep, flee the dark-limbed carcass's cold glance?
Only the mad, we think, may truly dance.

Ed Gein Critiques his Biopics

Down here in Hell, they've got a movie theatre
And in my copious free time, I'm aghast
To see my weird existence rendered weirder
The further it retreats into the past.

Though I liked *Psycho*, I'll give Hitchcock flack,
For I was sagging, plump, no Tony Perkins,
And he omitted my artistic bent, my knack
For slicing women's privates into merkins.

When *Texas Chainsaw Massacre* came out,
Trophies there were of skin and flesh and bone
Reminding me of home. What made me pout?
They had a clan – *I* did it all alone!

And ho-hum Hannibal? I just ignored
That Oscar and that Golden Globe Award.

John Wayne Gacy

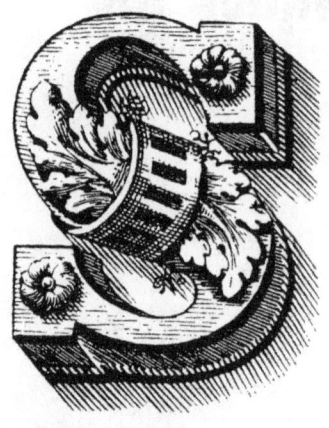

Sure, fuck me. I'm fifteen. I know
          the score,
Knew from the moment I
          stepped off that bus

From Cleveland. Bruise me? I'm already sore;
I've been a hustler since I learned to cuss

In seventh grade. It takes much more to scare
A dude like me than some scratched-up old
          knife,
A fat man in a clown suit, with a pair
Of handcuffs and no key -- shit, that's my life.

o, sonny, that's your death.
      You know so
           much,

You ought to recognize what's in my eyes;
Should have foreseen the meaning in my touch
And sensed somehow these weren't the same
           old lies.

Before your screaming is forever stilled,
I want to hear you beg me to be killed.

On a List of People at One Time Thought to be Jack the Ripper

Klosowski and Kosminksi come to mind
As Scotland Yard's thoughts race from Pole to Pole;
Ostrog, Pizer, Druitt one will find
Have been enlisted in the Ripper's rôle.

Sadler, Silver, Sickert, Stephen, Stephenson,
Cohen and Cutbush, Tumblety and Cream,
Chapman and Maybrick, Hutchinson and even some
Female names have joined the suspects' team.

Fanciful theorists fancy Lewis Caroll,
While monarchists believe the Duke of Clarence
Donning decidedly unposh apparel
Was getting back at too-Imperious parents.

They've scoured the world from Timbuktu to Sidney,
Yet one dead whore's still missing half a kidney.

Armin Meiwes: The Cannibal

    placed an ad; he answered;
        that is all.

    We had our ritual in a private room;
Both he and I in individual thrall
Each to his demon, each to his private doom.

The copious blood came as a slight surprise
And slicing clean took effort, strength, and will,
But on the dish I still could recognize
What oft I ate, yet ne'er before did grill.

O heavenly communion! We were one!
He was both bread and wine to me; and, slain,
He nourished me, rare, medium, and well done,
Enfolded me in sacrificial pain.

'Tis strange that legal precedents are tested
When all I did was what the man requested.

Albert Fish

"Why, you're a likely lad, young - is it Ed?
— Wait, I'll just slide a needle in my thigh —
Come into town — I'll give you work," he said,
"You'll be some use to me before you die."

"My gentleman's demeanor never fails
To calm them down, while I heat up the kettle
— Excuse me while I scarf some rusty nails —
For boys go well with shards of sharpened metal."

I've killed and snacked on, oh, a hundred kids,
While my six children never even guessed.
I torture, aim and hack as heaven bids:
God tells me who to eat — I do the rest.

But though I follow all my darkest urgings
I'm pure of sin — the children all die virgins.

II

Gay Bible Stories

Tinky Winky at the Televangelist's Tomb

hen Tinky Winky to the funeral went
      He kissed th' embalmed, rouged
           corpse upon each cheek.
Flexing his pink purse, by the bier
      he bent
And in limp-wristed googoo tones did
      speak:

"O, Jerry, Jerry, some have called you bigot
For outing me. And yet, to me, 'tis fate;
Once on, one cannot just turn off the spigot
Whence flows oppression, scorn, distrust
                      and hate.

You gave me too much credit. It's their
>   *genes*,
And not the influence of my vile
>   skulduggery
Upon the minds of pre-pre-pre-pre-teens
That turns those British babies' thoughts
>   to buggery.

You've made a noble effort to forestall hell:
In life you soared — in death, you did
>   not fall well."

Matthew Shepard

he church hath spoken.
                        'Tis in black and white.
The wages of your sin brook no exemption,
No bribe but blood can put the dark to flight;
A lamb must die that you may gain redemption.

But I was never reared to be that lamb,
Nor ever sought in martyrdom my joy;
I never craved the power to save or damn,
Nor asked to be your movement's poster boy.

ow is it then that I came to be chosen
Who now am pierced and crowned with thorns of steel,
Who now am scourged and in the chill night frozen,
Who feels, that one day you may learn to feel?

O God, did not one lamb suffice for Thee,
Who hangs a second Shepherd on Thy tree?

III

Women who Kill their own Children

Andrea Yates: on drowning my babies

Turn on the water in the Yates Motel

And suffer the little babes to come to Him.
The gates of heaven are a liquid hell
When Mother glowers by the bathtub's rim.

Now, Bethlehem in 4 BC was tense:
And yet that manger was a bed of roses
Next to the cradles of those innocents —
And — didn't Jewish babies die for Moses?

So — what's another five? thought Mrs. Yates
When angels brought her messages from Jesus.
Woman makes more, she thought, whene'er she
                mates;
She smiled and mused, See? It's the Truth that
                frees us.

Mysterious are the ways of God, you see;
Far too mysterious for the likes of me.

Deanna Schlosser:
on slicing off my baby's arms

A Plano Angel voiced a plain ol' truth:
When God commands, it's best he be obeyed.
Moses and Abraham, Job, Saul, and Ruth
All knew that sacrifices must be made.

Lord, how she screamed! Gore spurted
                              everywhere,
And all that mess! The blood started to thicken,
Clotting the kitchen counter and my hair.
I barely know how to debone a chicken!

And that, distinguished members of the jury,
Is why they hauled me up on filicide;
I sliced my daughter's arms off not in fury,
But in submission to God's will. (She died.)

9-1-1 was so sweet. Am I alarming
You nice good folks? God's voice was so …
                    disarming.

Susan Smith:
on driving her babies to the lake

Her memory mothers her, a
                    monstrous lake
That swallows up youth, truth, future and
            past
In its lactating presence. Every ache
It washes, soothes, locks out, rolls up, seals
            fast
Except the one ache which, like a black hole
Sucks at the soul itself. Her memory
            smothers,
Siphons away the air, lets the past roll
Till it submerges with a thousand others.

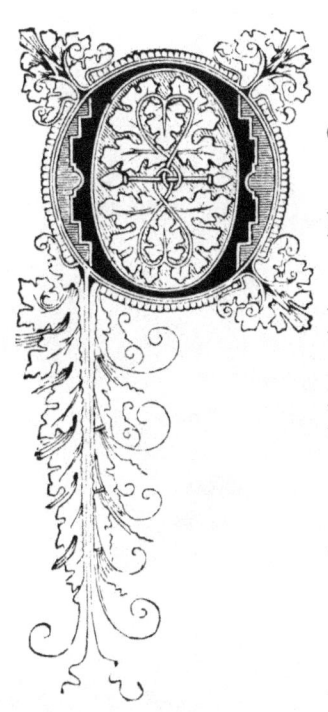 children of the cold, cold
        womb, entombed
In greatest, gravest darkness,
        do not weep;
For your frail tears can only
        be subsumed;
Nothing is more eternal than
        the deep --

"I pray the Lord," she cries,
        "their souls to
            take;
I pray the Lord they die
    before they wake."

IV

Mass Murderers

VI

Blacksburg

It's not my fault. *You* made me who I am,
Abused, reclused, and finally confused me.
So when that salesman didn't care a damn,
No shrinks, pleas, plays, or ploys could have defused me.

It ain't *my* fault. The law's 'bout plain as day,
And everything I'm told to tell, I tells 'em.
You can be psycho, wacko, schizo, mad, or gay —
That just ain't my department. I just sells 'em.

It's not *our* fault. We make these toys of steel
For recreation, not for retribution;
Statistics, demographics, can't conceal
The rights God granted in our constitution.

While everybody cries "For shame, for shame,"
Why is there nobody to take the blame?

Columbine

After the bloody dead were cleared
                      away
Floors waxed and wiped, bullet holes sanded flat,
Came thoughts far worse, even, than that dark day:
Recriminations. Explanations, that
Failed to explain away at all, but told
How helpless humans are, and how inapt
Are words, to mourn those who shall not grow old,
Their bright hopes dashed, dreams smashed: saplings,
                            unsapped.

Bullying can warp. Depression surely maims.
Blame a messiah complex more complex
Than Zoloft can assuage, or videogames.
These blandishments mask truths that ever vex:
How each life dies; how each bush hides its weavil;
Each good comes matched to corresponding evil.

V

Children who Kill their Parents

Alex King

I killed my daddy with a baseball bat
Then I burned down the house and ran away.
His brains squished out of him right where he sat
I thought, one less adult for me to obey.
There's just one grownup person in my life
Who really loves me, and his name is Rick,
So, maybe I can't really be his wife,
But still, at least, he lets me suck his dick.
There's nothing wrong with me, I'm just a victim;
The shrinks all tell me I was just confused,
I saw Rick's note from jail, *yeah!* we sure tricked 'em,
I know it's love. I know I'm not abused.
So what if I'm just 12? I watch TV.
I know that cute kids get away scot-free.

Erik Menendez

y father frequently had sex with me,
So I thought I should kill my mom ... as well.
A matched set satisfies one's sense of *chi*
Ensuring no divergent tales to tell.

You can't conceive what torments I went through,
To what privations I became inured.
Allowance cut, no BMW,
Oh. what capricious cruelties I endured!

If I were cute and poor, like blue-eyed Alex,
I wouldn't spend a second in the slammer;
You guys are just not into rich hispanics,
We should be drowned with drugs,
      not drenched in glamour.

I could have had my share of daddy's dough,
But now I'm spending life as Bubba's who'.

VI

Washington, DC

The Lewinsky Quartet

I: Monica Lewinsky

Twixt the grand summits and fundraising coffees
You come, soft, white, and rhyming with Stravinsky.
Your oval lips abuse my oval office,
Your dancing tongue, like a rotund Nijinsky
Scarfing me down, smooth, like a cheese blintz.
It's rough -- excuse the pun -- in my position
Despite the pundits' not so subtle hints --
To conjure up some semblance of contrition.
"How strange, when politics and love enmesh,"
I'm thinking as those lusty lips go down
With soft-ridged teeth to graze my surging flesh,
"How easy stands the head that wears a crown...."
Alas! Had I but rightly gauged the ratio
Of those who feel that sex is not fellatio!

The Lewinsky Quartet

II: To a Cigar

O leafy rod, born between dusky thighs,
That now shalt find a whiter, moister dwelling,
Couldst thou but know what ecstasy, what sighs
Thou hast inspired, and eke what rampant swelling
Within this fleshy rod, that yearns to be
Inside that selfsame cavity thou probest! --
That thou shouldst cause -- ah, such an irony! --
The downfall of the mightiest and the noblest!
For even now, in Bangkok, lit cigars
Are being used as props in nudie shows,
And tourists in a thousand sleazy bars
Gawk at clenched vulvas, and pay through the nose.
Next time, dear, we will try with a banana
To further build relations with Havana.

The Lewinsky Quartet

III: On a Copy of Leaves of Grass

Presented by the President to Miss Lewinsky

We're different, Mr. Whitman, if you please;
I'm very straight; you're absolutely out.
You sucked the dicks of teenage amputees,
And yet *your* legacy is not in doubt.
The pundits never let me out of sight,
They've even probed the presidential toilet;
Victorians were notoriously uptight,
Yet your life had no prurient snoops to spoil it.
How did you do it, Walt? It's a conundrum
They crucify me for one sultry lass
While your sex life's a thousand times less humdrum —
As anyone can see in Leaves of Grass.
For as professors have opined so well,
We never have to ask: you always tell.

The Lewinsky Quartet

IV: The Sky at Night

Number me not those thousand points of light!
    There are more Starrs in Washington, DC.
Peering through keyholes through the livelong night
Counting uncounted counts of perjury,
Tallying tales, and weighing verbiage,
Monica's girth, and Kathleen's breast cup size,
Attempting so scientifically to gauge
The whiteness of their thighs -- and of my lies.
When *stella nova* shines in heaven's dome
The downfall of great men is never far:
A comet prophesied the fall of Rome --
So aptly did they name thee, Mr. Starr.
She came to me with bright stars in her eyes;
But now, it seems, I have them in my flies.

A Congressional Page contemplates Mr. Foley's Proposition

knew up front that pages were fair game
That's why I joined. You *could* say I'm a sucker,
But there's no faster way to tabloid fame,
Unless you've talent, than the old "star fucker."
So, why *not* let him flirt with me a bit?
Oh, don't be so self-righteous. It's just sex,
Well, call me a self-centered little shit,
But I *like* compliments about my ass and pecs
And so would *any* horny teen my age.
He hints around about the ancient Greeks,
I smile and play the worshipful young page,
And think, "Ask me already! All this talk's for geeks."
Next year, with H.C. in da house, I'll pack
My presidential kneepads in my sack.

Mr. Foley contemplates the Internet

The *inter* makes you think, wide open spaces,
Millions of souls connected in a snap;
A cosmos full of trails that don't leave traces —
The *net* should tell you plain, it's all a trap.
Words typed can't be untyped. True, thoughts can be
Unthought, lust put aside, inapt desire
Suppressed in favor of the polity;
But one IM can rouse the world to ire.
Yet it's not for those barely legal teens
Who thought you just some lecherous old man;
All those reproaches, histrionic scenes,
Took place because you're a Republican.
Ah, foolish Foley! Cease your sordid chats!
Leave the fine art of sin to Democrats!

VI

Science Fiction

In Praise of Entropy

He warped out of some future Space and Time
And said: "'Tis wondrous, in this antique Land
That stone legs may stand trunkless in the Sand
And Transient Beauty is not deemed a crime
Evoking Public Censure. Where I live,
The Lifeless are Constrained to Permanence;
No sand may sift through Time's intemperate sieve.
Ten Thousand years, the Tall Titanium Tents
Remain unweathered by the Acid Rain.
Encased in force-fields, our proud Ziggurats
Will never shatter, for each window-pane
Is double-strapped with Diamantine slats.
How long, O Ozymandias, till the Earth
Learns this great truth: sans Death, there is no Birth?"

VII

Silly Sonnets on Serious Subjects

Moral Ambiguity in Thailand and Sudan

Thai women don't wear slacks on temple sites,
To not piss off the pious, or inflame
The appetites of our chaste cenobites,
   Or drown our morals-conscious town in shame.

But if a girl forgets, and dares to flaunt
A pair of jeans before our sacred Buddhas,
She's but to rent a skirt from those who haunt
The doorways, making money as do-gooders.

There's no such ambiguity in Khartoum,
Where pants in brasseries can be a pain,
The wrong attire can spell a woman's doom —
The lash for Lubna Ahmed al-Hussein!
If Christ got 39 for freeing man,
What's one more lash for freedom in Sudan?

On looking into a copy of Chapman's Homer
that might have belonged to Keats

hey stood in Darien, little knowing how
A poet would allude to them long thence.
Their lives as metaphor remembered now
More real than real, intenser than intense.

They came; they conquered; now they're gone. But I,
I too have held those pages, knowing Keats
As one might know the earth, or sea, or sky,
A pillar of my world. Against deceits,
And disillusions, and entropic fears,
Beauty and truth do blend a powerful potion.
My tired corpus piqued by time and tears,
I stand on Keats and see a farther ocean
Where Darien itself stands not, or ever
Silent, for the tide flows backwards never.

George Junius Stinney
(1929-1944)
the youngest American executed in the electric chair in the United States in the 20th Century

"He done it," Mary Emma sister say.
"E'er'body know, before that trial they know
He done it." Didn't need no trial. I pray
They be a trial *up there*, where nex' I go.
Cuz I the younges' one to get the chair
I get a footnote in that true crime book.
I just fourteen and so it don't seem fair
When white boys allus just gets off the hook.

Too young? "Oh, nigger, you too black to live.
At five feet tall, you ain't too small to kill,
They tells me, and you too old to forgive."
Them girls was sweet. I wish they done held still.
Them girls dead now. I ain't too young to die,
Cuz now they killing me, I don't know why.

A Prime Example of Why the Sonnet is not the Ideal Medium for the Lyrics of Popular Music

n sooth, *how many roads* must one walk down

Before a man *a man* may callèd be?
Before she layeth on the sand her crown,
Must a white *dove* sail over many a sea?

How oft must cannon *balls* fly o'er the land
(Wait, hold that rhyme, it's not yet time for that)
Before they must eternally be *banned*?
(*Now* comes that damn rhyme — drat,
              and double drat!)

Six lines I've left to squeeze in all the rest,
The *ears*, the *mountains*, and the *seeing blind*,
Erosion, *deaths*, *head-turning*, *freedom*, lest
We do forget, the *blowing in the wind**.
I prithee, Mr. Dylan, think upon it
And cast thy lines in other than a *sonnet*.

*to be pronounced as in Shakespeare's "Blow, thou winter wind."

Trivializing Götterdämmerung

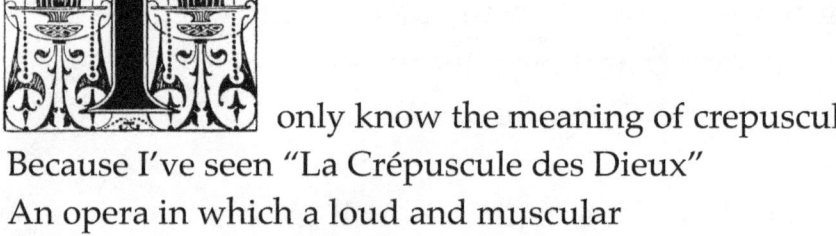only know the meaning of crepuscular
Because I've seen "La Crépuscule des Dieux"
An opera in which a loud and muscular
Soprano brings on cosmic "malheureux."

But Wagner, sung in French, becomes debatable,
And one must give the Teutons their just due;
For German words, when Frenched, become inflatable,
And all those twanging vowels don't "ring" true.

Italians, more peninsular in attitude,
Don't bother to translate "The Ring" at all –
For operagoers there, romantic platitude,
Not deep philosophy, holds them in thrall.

If from polluted language you'd be free,
Move to an island that has no TV.

Appendix

Sonetti su serial killers
Traduzioni di Paolo Maurizio Bottigelli & Vittorio Curtoni

I would like to append these lovely translations of four of my pieces, done by two brilliant Italians, which were published years ago in an Italian webzine.

I've heard of a Hebrew translation as well, but I've never been able to get hold of it.

Jeffrey Dahmer

La morte è una minuscola puntura.
Soltanto un'iniezione.
Nulla da temere. Nè sofferenza, nè dolore
Di fronte alla dura, stupefacente pugnalata
Della solitudine. L'acido che corre al cervello
Scioglierà il residuo d'orrore;
Poi, d'un tratto, per volontà dall'alto,
La trascendenza; e desiderio, torrenti tempestosi.
Per te, eterno amore;
Per me, caducità; perché divoro
E ciò ch'era bello si muta in vecchie ossa
E carne, a marcire in una stanza di periferia,
Mentre la tua risposta ai miei gemiti continui
È il non parlare affatto. Ma resta, resta!
Non come gli altri: il vero amore ignora la putrefazione!

Susan Smith

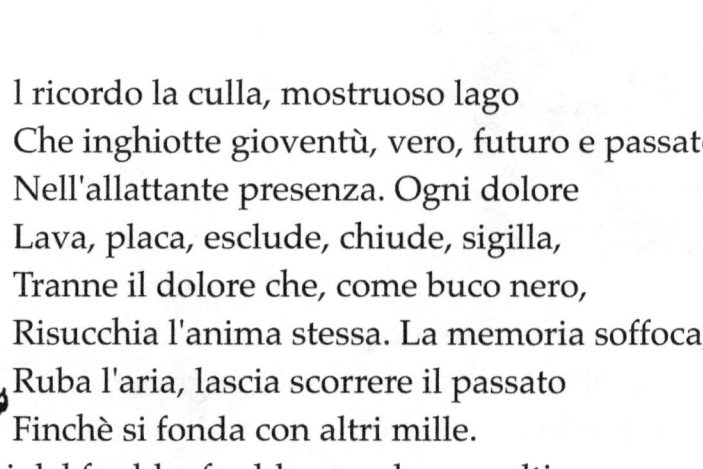

I ricordo la culla, mostruoso lago
Che inghiotte gioventù, vero, futuro e passato
Nell'allattante presenza. Ogni dolore
Lava, placa, esclude, chiude, sigilla,
Tranne il dolore che, come buco nero,
Risucchia l'anima stessa. La memoria soffoca,
Ruba l'aria, lascia scorrere il passato
Finchè si fonda con altri mille.
Bambini del freddo, freddo grembo, sepolti
Nella grande, greve oscurità, più non piangete;
Le vostre fragili lacrime vanno recintate;
Nulla è piu' eterno dell'abisso...
"Prego il Signore" lei urla "che prenda l'anima loro;
Prego il Signore che muoiano prima di svegliarsi."

Ed Gein

uel brulichio di donna sul suo sesso così
caloroso,
I capezzoli strappati a raggrupparsi sul
suo petto d'uomo,
Lui danzava. Con monili d'ossa di donne senza tempo
Tintinnati, risonanti; e con vesti di carni
Femminili rigide e lucenti, danzava. Solo
Sotto la morta luna del Wisconsin, danzava,
Passando da ragazza a madre, a vecchia;
Clown in un semplice schermo, ma trafitto da un'antica
Profonda magia, prime tracce, filamenti di fuoco,
Brillava. Il mondo come passato, in questa danza?
Potremmo anche noi danzare, come storie con la paura
d'essere mutati in pietra
Da questo mondo non inventato che ci spinge ad amare,
ridere, soffrire,
Piangere, fuggire al freddo sguardo della nera carcassa?
Soltanto il folle, pensiamo, può veramente danzare.

John Wayne Gacy

ottimi. Ne ho quindici di anni. Il prezzo lo conosco,
Scritto nel momento che sono sceso da quel bus
Da Cleveland. Lividi? Sono colori notturni sulla carne
Di puttana, puttana da che ho imparato a bestemmiare.
Per spaventare uno come me
Non basta un vecchio coltello un po' del cazzo,
Un ciccione vestito da clown, con un paio
Di manette senza chiavi. La mia vita! E sono in una vita
 di merda.

No, figliolo, è la tua morte. E così sai?
Dovresti riconoscere quel che ho negli occhi;
Non vedi il senso del contatto?
Parla alla tua mente, dille che non erano le solite
 vecchie bugie.
Prima che il tuo urlo si plachi per sempre,
Voglio sentirti implorare ch'io t'uccida.

End Notes
The Historical Context

End Notes

By definition, the tabloids are here today and gone tomorrow. Because of this, I'm providing a few end notes to this little book. On the off chance that all civilization is destroyed and this slim volume is all that remains, it would be nice to have a few simple explanations about what the hell is going on, and who these supposedly famous, and infamous, subjects of the sonnets might have once been.

Ed Gein was a remarkable character. He lived in Wisconsin, and his life story inspired many films, including *Psycho* and *The Texas Chainsaw Massacre*. When Robert Bloch wrote the novel *Psycho*, much of the psychological analysis of Norman Bates was Bloch's own brilliant speculation based on the few facts one could glean from newspaper reports at the time. Bloch's interpretation of the character proved uncannily accurate.

Jeffrey Dahmer killed and ate young men, not because he really wanted them to die per se; he had a desperate need not to be abandoned.

John Wayne Gacy dressed as a clown and visited children in hospitals; he also picked up boys at bus stops and tortured them horribly. An interesting feature of his madness is that he only killed people who *asked* to be killed, which they would inevitably do if the pain reached a certain level. At least one person managed to escape because he didn't ask for death....

Arwin Meiwes killed and ate someone after running an ad to find someone who wanted to be killed and eaten. They cooked and shared the victim's penis. Arwin wasn't punished because the victim's death was technically an assisted suicide, rather than murder, and the existence of crime such as this had never been predicted by any lawmaker in his native Germany; it therefore had never been legislated against....

One of the Teletubbies, named *Tinky Winky*, is purple and appears to carry a purse. Televangelist Jerry Falwell inveighed against this indoctrination of the gay lifestyle into the minds of young children. His polemics raised the gay Teletubby to the status of an icon.

Matthew Shephard, too, has become an icon. But I don't believe he would have wanted to exchange his life for it.

The four women who killed their own children did so for various reasons: one wanted to rid herself of impediments to a boyfriend, another heard the voices of angels. It's worth noting that in other cultures in history, it was quite acceptable for parents to off their own kids; the Roman *paterfamilias* had the right of life and death over his children, and people everywhere in the ancient world exposed their babies to be eaten by wild beasts if they could not bring them up. Obviously these women were just born in the wrong century....

The Blacksburg mass murderer was notable because he killed a holocaust survivor. He also killed the son of a friend of mine, the novelist Michael Bishop. And everyone blamed someone else.

Columbine is famous for massacres: there is *another* one from 1927, in which police killed unarmed striking miners in a town called Serene, Colorado.

Alex King was a sweet boy of eleven or twelve who fell in love with one Ricky Chavis, and he and his brother ended up killing their father and burning down the house. Ricky was just your average predator, and probably didn't quite know what hit him when these boys went over the edge. Tried as adults and hideously sentenced, the boys eventually were freed through the efforts of celebs like Rosie O'Donnell,

When I wrote the *Lewinsky Quartet*, it seemed that Monica Lewinsky would never need an introduction, yet much water has flowed under that bridge. It is perhaps worth a reminder that this Rubensesque young lady was an intern at the White House and that she famously almost brought down the presidency and was, for months, the focus of national attention as the somewhat tawdry details of the romance came to light. Things like cum-stained dresses, the phallic use of cigars, and the expression "presidential kneepads" became iconic in the popular consciousness.

Mark Foley's dalliances with congressional pages has also, perhaps, been consigned tabloid oblivion, but here too the public was mystified to discover that their representatives in government had feet of clay - not to mention penises.

In Sudan, a woman named *Lubna Ahmed al-Hussein* received forty lashes for wearing trousers. In Thailand, people are also expected to dress respectably in certain places like temples, but simple sarongs are always available for rent at the entrance. The idea of whipping people for being inappropriately dressed is quite shocking in this Buddhist country.

Chapman's *Homer* was an iconic book that influenced many people, and I was fortunate enough to come within inches of it in the Eton College Library when my brilliant mentor, Michael Meredith, showed it to me one day, forty years after I was at school there.

George Stinney was the youngest person ever executed in the electric chair in America. The trial was tinged with racism and he may well have been completely innocent, or at least so not "right in the head" that he had no idea what was going on.

Bob Dylan wrote the iconic song the lyrics of which I attempted unsuccessfully to put into sonnet from. A reminder of the inadequacy of translation when it comes to high art of any kind....

I wrote the final poem in this book only because I was asked to use "crepuscular" in a sentence.

About the Author

Once referred to by the *International Herald Tribune* as "the most well-known expatriate Thai in the world," Somtow Sucharitkul is no longer an expatriate, since he has returned to Thailand after five decades of wandering the world. He is best known as an award-winning novelist and a composer of operas.

Born in Bangkok, Somtow grew up in Europe and was educated at Eton and Cambridge. His first career was in music and in the 1970s he acquired a reputation as a revolutionary composer, the first to combine Thai and Western instruments in radical new sonorities. Conditions in the arts in the region at the time proved so traumatic for the young composer that he suffered a major burnout, emigrated to the United States, and reinvented himself as a novelist.

His earliest novels were in the science fiction field but he soon began to cross into other genres. In his 1984 novel Vampire Junction, he injected a new literary inventiveness into the horror genre, in the words of Robert Bloch, author of Psycho, "skillfully combining the styles of Stephen King, William Burroughs, and the author of the Revelation to John." Vampire Junction was voted one of the forty all-time greatest horror books by the Horror Writers' Association, joining established classics like Frankenstein and Dracula.

In the 1990s Somtow became increasingly identified as a uniquely Asian writer with novels such as the semi-autobiographical Jasmine Nights. He won the World Fantasy Award, the highest accolade given in the world of fantastic literature, for his novella The Bird Catcher. His fifty-three books have sold about two million copies worldwide.

After becoming a Buddhist monk for a period in 2001, Somtow decided to refocus his attention on the country of his birth, founding Bangkok's first international opera company and returning to music, where he again reinvented himself, this time as a neo-Asian neo-Romantic composer. The Norwegian government commissioned his song cycle Songs Before Dawn for the 100th Anniversary of the Nobel Peace Prize, and he composed at the request of the government of Thailand his Requiem: In Memoriam 9/11 which was dedicated to the victims of the 9/11 tragedy.

According to London's Opera magazine, "in just five years, Somtow has made Bangkok into the operatic hub of Southeast Asia." His operas on Thai themes, Madana, Mae Naak, and Ayodhya, have been well received by international critics. His most recent opera, The Silent Prince, was premiered in 2010 in Houston, and a fifth opera, Dan no Ura, will premiere in Thailand in the 2013 season. His sixth opera, Midsummer, will premiere in the UK in 2014.

He is increasingly in demand as a conductor specializing in opera and in the late-romantic composers like Mahler. His repertoire runs the entire gamut from Monteverdi to Wagner. His work has been especially lauded for its stylistic authenticity and its lyricism. The orchestra he founded in Bangkok, the Siam Philharmonic, is mounting the first complete Mahler cycle in the region.

He is the first recipient of Thailand's "Distinguished Silpathorn" award, given for an artist who has made and continues to make a major impact on the region's culture, from Thailand's Ministry of Culture.

Books by S. P. Somtow

General Fiction

The Shattered Horse
Jasmine Nights
Forgetting Places
The Other City of Angels (Bluebeard's Castle)
The Stone Buddha's Tears

Dark Fantasy

The Timmy Valentine Series:
Vampire Junction
Valentine
Vanitas

Moon Dance
Darker Angels
The Vampire's Beautiful Daughter

Science Fiction

Starship & Haiku
Mallworld
The Ultimate Mallworld

Chronicles of the High Inquest:
Light on the Sound
The Darkling Wind
The Throne of Madness
Utopia Hunters
Chroniques de l'Inquisition - Volume 1 (omnibus)
Chroniques de l'Inquisition - Volume 2 (omnibus)

The Aquiliad Series:
Aquila in the New World
Aquila and the iron Horse
Aquila and the Sphinx

Fantasy

The Riverrun Trilogy:
Riverrun
Armorica
Yestern
The Riverrun Trilogy (omnibus)

The Fallen Country
Wizard's Apprentice

Media Tie-in

V: The Alien Swordmaster
V: Symphony of Terrror
The Crow: Temple of Night
Star Trek: Do Comets Dream?

Chapbooks

Fiddling for Waterbuffaloes
I Wake from a Dream of a Drowned Star City
A Lap Dance with the Lobster Lady
Compassion: Two Perspectives

Libretti

Mae Naak
Ayodhya
Madana
The Silent Prince
Dan no Ura
Chui Chai
Helena Citronova

Collections

My Cold Mad Father
Fire from the Wine Dark Sea
Chui Chai (Thai)
Nova (Thai)
The Pavilion of Frozen Women
Dragon's Fin Soup
Tagging the Moon
Face of Death (Thai)
Other Edens
S.P. Somtow's The Great Tales (Thai)
Other Edens
Bible Stories for Secular Humanists

Essays, Poetry and Miscellanies

Opus Fifty
A Certain Slant of "I"
Sonnets about Serial Killers
Opera East
Victory in Vienna
Nirvana Express

S.P. SOMTOW TITLES
AVAILABLE FROM DIPLODOCUS PRESS

THE INQUESTOR TETRALOGY

Somtow's far-flung galactic civilization is a creation to rival Silverberg's *Majipoor* or Herbert's *Dune*. It is a universe with its own language and exotic customs, vividly etched characters and rich history that spans thousands of worlds and tens of thousands of years.

The godlike Inquestors of the High Inquest had forsaken all that made them human. But one young Inquestor rediscovered the power of compassion and hastened the end of their ancient, starflung empire....

"In a prose that evokes the spirited imagination of the symbolist painters and poets, Somtow postulates a complex universe of immense scope ... upholds the author's place as one of SF's formidable talents." – Publishers Weekly

Light on the Sound ISBN 978-09800149-9-0
The Throne of Madness ISBN 978-09800149-2-1
Utopia Hunters ISBN 978-09800149-8-3
The Darkling Wind ISBN 978-09900142-0-1

S.P. SOMTOW TITLES
AVAILABLE FROM DIPLODOCUS PRESS

THE TIMMY VALENTINE SERIES

Available for the first time in a uniform edition since their original publication, the classic *Vampire Junction* series is now acknowledged as one of the most important classics of twentieth-century gothic literarture, S.P. Somtow's tale of a twelve-year-old rock star vampire, his Jungian analyst, and the Wagnerian conductor who is his nemesis turned the entire genre upside down in the 1980s and is considered the ancestor of the "splatterpunk" movement. Vampire Junction has been voted one of the top forty horror books of all time. Timmy Valentine: "He'll steal your heart - and have it for breakfast!" 21st anniversary edition of this unforgettable classic of high-intensity horror.

". . . It's about rock music, about mass hysteria, about vampires, about horror . . . one comes out knowing, and caring, about a panoply of new friends and acquaintances, living and dead, and unalive".--Theodore Sturgeon, The Washington Post.

Vampire Junction trade paperback $21   978-08125259-6-0
Valentine trade paperback $25.50   978-09800149-6-9
Vanitas trade paperback $27   978-09800149-7-6

COMING IN 2014

P.D. Cacek's *Visitation Rites*

He's here....

"Did either of us tell you that our lovely, wonderful home is haunted?"

P.D. Cacek does ghosts like nobody else, and *Visitation Rites* is classic Cacek. Inspired by real-life locations in the Revolutionary War in which a battle was lost by the Colonials, the novel's spooky setting in a rural Pennsylvania estate, its quirky, unforgettable characters, create a richly atmospheric book that will leave with the reader for a long time afterwards.

hardcover 978-1-940999-01-2
trade paperback 978-1-940999-00-5

www.ingramcontent.com/pod-product-compliance
Lightning Source LLC
Chambersburg PA
CBHW020015050426
42450CB00005B/481